THE ABBA CRY

What is the loudest voice within you?

BY DON LESSIN

Son Gaze

PUBLICATIONS

P.O. Box 6947
Siloam Springs, Arkansas 72761

Scripture taken from the Holy Bible, King James Version.

Scripture taken from the Holy Bible,
New Living Translation copyright © 1996 by permission
of Tyndale House Publishers, Inc., Wheaton, IL.
www.newlivingtranslation.com

ISBN 0-9767316-0-6

First Printing 2005
Second Printing 2009

Printed in the United States of America

Cover photo by Craig Stewart Studio
Book design by Lorinda Gray/The Ragamuffin Acre

www.songaze.com

This booklet contains edited transcripts of two sermons that were preached by Don Lessin at Outreach Center in Northwest Arkansas. The messages were originally titled Abba and Three Questions in the Spirit. The truths in each message were powerfully used by God to draw people closer to His heart. It is our prayer that as you read, your heart will also be drawn closer to His.

THE ABBA CRY

"For as many as are led by the Spirit of God, they are the sons of God. For ye have not received the spirit of bondage again to fear; but ye have received the Spirit of adoption, whereby we cry, Abba, Father."

ROMANS 8:14-15 KJV

The Abba Cry

PART ONE

The Beautiful Sound of His Name

IT IS IMPORTANT FOR YOU TO LISTEN to what is going on inside you. It is there in the deepest part of your being that your walk with the Lord begins and continues. Often there are many sounds that we hear within us. As we listen to these sounds, we can hear the voice of our own thoughts and opinions, we can hear the voices of others, and we can hear the voice of the Holy Spirit speaking to us. In the midst of all these sounds, what is the deepest sound you hear? What is the loudest, clearest, and strongest voice within you?

Many believers today know little of the depths of His voice speaking within them. God desires for us to open our spiritual ears and to listen to what the voice of His Spirit is speaking within us. He wants you to listen to what He is saying about your motives, your desires, your longings, your attitudes, your priorities, and your responses toward Him.

The Bible says that the Holy Spirit within us is crying "Abba, Father," and that we, as adopted sons and daughters, cry and say "Abba, Father." The voice of the Holy Spirit is always crying "Abba, Father." That sound is the voice of intimacy. It is the sound that should be the loudest sound within us. At this moment, from the deepest part of who we are, should come the cry, "Abba, Father."

What is the loudest sound that you hear within you? What is the sound that rings the loudest day in and day out? Have you been quiet enough in your inner man to know? That doesn't necessarily mean being on your knees for ten hours a day, but it means getting quiet enough to hear the dominant sounds that are going on within you. The loudest sounds that you hear and listen to are the true indicators of what is really happening in your spiritual walk. What you do and the choices you make are by-products of what is going on within you.

If you are married, it is a beautiful thing to hear within you the sound of your wife or husband. If you are a parent, it is wonderful to hear the sound of the children you love. Some hear the sounds of career and business, while others hear the sounds of ministry and church. All of these sounds can be good and right in their place, but none of these sounds should ring the loudest within us. We must go deeper and ask, "In my desires, in my ambitions, in the things I long to see fulfilled, what is the loudest sound I hear?"

What sound rings the loudest in the very center of your being? Is it Jesus? Is it "Abba, Father"? Can you really say, whatever your age, whatever your circumstance, that apart from all the good and beautiful sounds that you hear within you, Jesus' voice rings loudest? If there is another sound within you that takes the place of or weakens the sound of "Abba, Father" then that sound becomes idolatry. When anything else becomes the center of your being, when work or ministry, husband or wife, or son or daughter becomes the center of your being, then it is time to re-examine your heart's deepest priorities and affections.

At school, at work, at play, the sound that rings the loudest within you should be Abba, Abba, Abba, Abba, Father—that's who I live for!

Nothing Can Take His Place

Jesus must never become the means to an end. If your self-interests are the loudest sound within you, Jesus will become a means to that end. We may never admit it outwardly, but in our hearts we will know if Jesus is no longer the end we live for. If human relations take the place of Jesus, those relationships will become the loudest sound within you. Christian ministry can become the loudest sound that you hear. Ministry, marvelous ministry, can move Jesus into the shadows, even in the midst of working hard for Him.

A brother I had never seen before showed up in the church I was leading in Mexico. He had a word from the Lord for me. He began by saying, "This is a beautiful move of God here." He then waved a finger in my face and said, "Brother, I don't know you, but I have a message from the Lord for you. You give and you give and you give, but you need to get quiet because you've got some receiving to do. Jesus has some important things that He wants to say to you." I received the brother's word and thanked him for speaking it. I also thanked the Lord that He cared enough about me to bring that word to my heart. However, I confess to you that I did nothing about it. I simply went about my business of being busy for the Lord.

As time passed the burdens and responsibilities of the ministry continued to grow. Our church became the largest evangelical work in the state where I was living. God was moving in mighty ways during that time. I carried more and more of the responsibility in leadership, preaching, teaching, and counseling. It was a tremendous privilege to be a part of what God was doing. To an outsider, everything looked and seemed wonderful. However, things began to happen in my inner man. During those days when the work became so demanding I would often run into the presence of God and cry out, "Oh,

Lord, the pressure is on (and it was on). I need a word of direction. I need a word from You. I need to lead Your people, I need to disciple, I need to teach, I need to preach, and I need to counsel."

As time went by, my prayers of desperation were repeated. I'd continue to rush into the presence of God and say, "Lord, let me have a quick word from You. There's no time and there's so much to do. Sunday is coming up, and there's a leadership meeting tomorrow." In my hurried state, God was merciful to me. He would answer my prayers of desperation and give me the answers I sought. By His mercy He would continue to speak through me to others. When the teaching, preaching, and anointing were needed, God was there to minister to the needs of His people. I would thank Him a thousand times over for His mercy. In the midst of it all, however, something was happening to me. Walking in and out of the presence of God, and looking to Him for quick answers, I found that Jesus had become the means to an end. I began to lose out in the inner man.

The reality is that it is possible to be active in God's work, be used by Him to touch His people, and at the same time be losing out in the inner man. As a spiritual leader, the loudest sound within my being was ministry, responsibility, getting things done for God, preaching the right message, and saying the right thing. I was doing so much for Jesus while He was becoming secondary within me. "Can this be happening?" I wondered. "Can I be standing in a pulpit under the anointing of God and talking about Him while He becomes the secondary sound that I hear in the center of my being?" Sadly, the answer was "Yes."

I remembered the brother God sent to me, who warned me that I needed to get quiet before God. But, at the same time, I rationalized that I didn't have time to get quiet. I thought I was too busy to hear what was going on within me. Soon, inner frustration entered into my spirit. Emptiness began to crowd its way into my heart. Lack of satisfaction in what I was doing settled over me. Why? Because as I gave myself to the "marvelous ministry" I was a part of, I was drying up inside. In the midst of it all, Jesus was no longer at the center of my being. Abba, Father was no longer the loudest sound within me. I never ceased loving and serving Him, but He was not the center of my being. Ministry took His place. Ministry rang louder in my heart; ministry had taken His place. One day I looked around at all that was going on and became bored with all.

Is Jesus Really Enough?

I know from experience and from the testimony of others that people in the midst of revival and with the blessing of God upon their families can become empty inside because Jesus is not the sound that rings the loudest within them. Can you be honest about what is really going on inside you? What do you think about the most? It's one thing to have hobbies or be good at your job, but in the midst of those things what sound rings the loudest within you? Is it Abba? Is it Jesus? Does He really matter? Do you really care that He be glorified in what you do from day to day? When you pray, does it really matter that He be glorified in the answer? Does it really matter that Jesus be glorified in your daily life, and that He be at the very center of your thinking? Is it important to you that He be lifted up? From the depths of your heart is your cry, "Father, I desire to walk more intimately with You?" Is He first place and at the center place of who you are and all you do?

A young man who was very organized and systematic in his thinking approached me one day after a church service. "I thought I had the Christian life all figured out," he said, "I figured if I gave so many hours to my job, so many hours to school, so many hours to my home life, and so many hours to Jesus, everything about my Christian life would work out perfectly." He then went on to add, "You know, it's never really worked. I've never really been satisfied in my inner man. The sounds of other things cry louder within me than the sound of Jesus." What that young man discovered was that it never works to have Jesus pushed to a corner of your heart. It never works to give Jesus a portion of who you are or a piece of what you do. Jesus has come to be at the very center of who you are and all you do. It is not wrong to organize your day, to work, to study, and to have friends, but all of these things must be the outflow of Jesus' presence within you. His voice must be the loudest sound you hear within you. His love must fill the deepest part of who you are. When Jesus is at the center, all the other things in your life will work out beautifully and be in their proper place.

Jesus is the Way. He is not only the Way to God, but He is the Way into all that God has for us. He is the Way into our devotions, to our Bible reading, to our prayer life, to our ministry, and to all that we do for Him. In reality, we do not do our work for Him, but He does His work through us. With Jesus in the center of our being, we are no longer victims of our expectations, circumstances, and the things we can't control. We discover that it's okay if people don't meet our expectations, because Jesus is our expectation. Schedules may be good, but they don't produce life within us because Jesus is our life.

Often, when my wife is working in the house, I hear a soft and tender sound coming from her inmost being. In the midst of doing dishes, ironing clothes, or when she is hurrying about to get something done, I hear the word "Jesus" being spoken. It's a sound that I'll hear over and over again. I don't know what she's thinking, I don't know if she's frustrated, praying, or rejoicing, but the thing that comes from her spirit is "Jesus." While being a mother, a wife, and a servant of the Lord, "Jesus" is the loudest sound within her. I remember something my wife shared a long time ago. She said, "My husband is not the most important person in my life—he never has been, nor will he ever be. Jesus is the most important thing in my life." That has made her the best wife I could ever have, because I'm not number one and I'm not the loudest sound in her spirit. In her spirit it's Jesus, it's Abba, and as a result she is the best wife that I could possibly have. I never want to be the loudest voice in her spirit; it would ruin things if I became the loudest voice within her heart. It would ruin our home.

In my own situation, as the sound of "Jesus" was replaced by the sound of ministry, I found that I began to have bad judgment as a father. Soon I ran into some problems with my oldest daughter. I was not living in any outward sin, but my thinking began to get off-center. I was embracing the work of the Lord but not the Lord of the work. I was being overcome with ministry, pressure, and responsibility. The sound within me was, "Do it, get the job done, say the right words, be the man of God." Wanting to be a man of God can be a dangerous thing. When people label you a man of God, when your work is labeled as a marvelous ministry, when you're called a success, it can be dangerous. Jesus is the only one who can keep you out of danger. All that you do has to be about all that He is. In the end, He will not throw His crown before us, but we will throw our crowns before Him. He alone is worthy. It's all for Him, it is all done through Him, and it all returns back to Him. Jesus is the center, the end, the beginning, and the great I AM. Day in and day out, in all we do, in all we say, the cry within us has to be "Jesus."

For five years the ministry I was involved in was the best. It was tremendous to disciple so many people for those five years. The day came, however, when God said "Out. Your time has come to an end." When I heard God's word to me, I obeyed. When I stepped away from the ministry, God directed me to be quiet before Him. For months I did nothing but wait before Him. No meetings, no preaching, no counseling.

It was during this time that I realized even more that it's possible to be busy in a prosperous work of God and be drying up on the inside. Can that really happen? Can we be doing more in His name and at the same time know Him less? The answer is "Yes." We can sing, worship and praise the Lord Sunday after Sunday, we can listen to Christian music and read Christians books, we can be raised in a Christian home, and still have the voice of Jesus be a distant sound within us.

Is Jesus what you really want? Is He enough? After 20 years in the ministry I had to ask myself these questions, or rather, God was asking them of me. It's not that ministry is wrong, or that having a beautiful family is wrong, but these things should be an outflow of our passion for Him. Is "Abba" what you really want in the center of your being? Way down deep, do you hear the voice of the Spirit of God talking to your spirit and saying, "Abba, Father?" Do you hear God saying, "Turn off all the sounds within you, but My voice. Turn off the sound of business, family, and ministry. Turn off the TV, the radio, and the music. Turn off the call of sports and movies and entertainment. Let it all be silent within you, and hear My voice"? As you listen to His voice what do you hear? Do you hear the Spirit saying, "Are you satisfied with Jesus? Are you really interested in taking time to be beautiful inside?" I encourage you to get quiet before Him today and nail down in your spirit what is the loudest sound that you want to hear.

PART TWO

Three Important Questions For Your Heart To Answer

In Job 38:1-3 God spoke these words, "Then the Lord answered Job from the whirlwind: "Who is this that questions My wisdom with such ignorant words? Brace yourself, because I have some questions for you, and you must answer them." Job 38:1-3 NLT

I would like you to consider some important questions that I believe are from the heart of God to each of us who hear the cry of Abba within. God's questions are not limited to our age or to our spiritual maturity. God has always used questions to reveal His heart to us, and His questions are also designed to reveal what is in us. He uses questions to help us see if there is harmony between our hearts and His. Recently I have heard God asking me some questions in the depths of my spirit. They were questions that I knew God wanted me to answer. His questions came to reveal not only what was in my heart toward Him, but also to reveal what was in my heart toward others.

QUESTION ONE:
How Much Do You Care About God's Feelings?

One of the questions that God asked me was, "What about My feelings? To what degree do My feelings really interest you?" What a deep impact that question has had on me. This is a question that I believe God will ask each of us as we seek His heart and want to know His voice. His questions and our responses can bring about a beautiful work within us.

There are times when we have questions of our own that we want to ask God. When we do, we often discover that He will answer our questions with a question. A brother in Christ once shared the following story with me. "I was going through a time when I experienced many injustices. I felt that I was wronged and people didn't understand me. Things went from bad to worse and my reputation was at stake. I came before the Lord and said, 'Lord, Lord, what about my reputation? Don't you care about my reputation?' The answer that I received from the Lord was a question back. He asked, 'What about My reputation? Do you care about My reputation? Do you not realize that you represent Me when you speak, when you act, and when you express your thoughts and attitudes in your daily walk?'"

QUESTION TWO:
To What Degree Can You Function Without God's Approval?

Here is a second important question that I want you to consider in your relationship with God. "To what degree can you function without His approval?" To what degree can you function as a father or mother, as a husband or wife, as a worker, or as a friend without the approval of God? In the crossroads of life, in important decisions, in your relationships with others, do you really care what God thinks? Do you ever ask God what He thinks about the decisions and choices you are making in your life? To what degree can you function without your Father's approval? When you can honestly open up your spirit to the Father with this question on your heart, you will find some very exciting things happening within you.

It is spiritually freeing when we come before the only One who truly knows us and ask Him to reveal our hearts to us. When we do, we don't have to devaluate ourselves or defend ourselves. We can simply ask Him to show us where we really are in our walk with Him. It doesn't matter if there are defects or imperfections involved. We seek to know where we are in Him because we care about His being glorified in our lives. We ask because what is on His heart matters to us.

Sometimes we are fearful of opening up our spirits to God because we think we will only hear how bad everything is within us. However, God loves to reveal the good things that are happening within us. There are many things that are so right and so beautiful in the inner man because of what God is doing in you and through you for His glory. He delights in showing you that you are growing, that you are a different person, and that the desires way down in your spirit have been placed there by His mercy and by His grace. You're not the same person that you were when you first knew Him, and you are not who you will be as He continues to move you on from glory to glory.

When God asked me the question, "To what degree can you function without my approval?" it penetrated deep within my spirit. I thought on it often before I could give an answer. One day the answer came ringing out from the deepest part of me, "Father, I cannot live without your approval. I just can't." There was a time in my walk with God when that wouldn't have been my answer. There was a time when I could function without His approval in how I lived my life. I thank Him for His mercy, and I thank Him that He is doing something in me that allows me to say at this moment "I cannot live without His approval." As a father, as a husband, as a servant of the Lord, and as your brother in Christ, I cannot live without His approval—I can't function without His approval; I can't make decisions without

His approval; I can't live without His blessing; I can't live without knowing that He is approving of my decisions; I can't function without knowing that He is approving of my relationships with others.

When I honestly answered the question that God asked me, I discovered something else. I found that I could live without the approval of others. If someone wrongly judges me, or dislikes me, or disapproves of my obedience to what God is asking of me, I can move on without that person's approval. I have found that living for God's approval has freed me from the bondage of trying to live for the approval of others. I desire the approval of others, I desire their love, I desire their fellowship, I desire their backing, I desire to walk hand in hand with others in the presence of the Lord, but if I can't, for whatever reason, I can still live in peace if I know I have His approval.

Can you really function without God's approval? Do you ask God what He thinks? If you are a young person, do you care what God thinks about your relationship with your boyfriend or girlfriend? If you are married, do you care what God thinks about how you treat your spouse? In your decisions in life, do you ask Him what He thinks before you do it? Do you seek His approval before you get involved, before you make commitments, before you take action?

Christianity is a relationship with God. It is not a system. If it's not a relationship, then it isn't anything—it's just form and ritual. God has called you to a relationship with Him, with His Son, and with His Holy Spirit. God wants you to be in a right relationship with Him; a relationship that gladdens His heart and receives His approval. The deeper that relationship becomes, the deeper will be your desire to live with His smile upon you. More and more you will long for the seal of His approval upon your decisions, and upon what you are doing and saying in your daily walk.

Some of God's people have developed a careless way of living. They go out and do things without seeking God's approval, and then go crying to God to fix the mess they've created. There are too many who desire His gifts, His benefits, and His prosperity, but do not desire His approval. I find it sad that this treasure of the heart is rare among God's people. Oh, the beauty upon a person who has a growing relationship with Jesus Christ, and who is daily seeking His approval—it is a treasure, a beautiful pearl!

QUESTION THREE:
How Many People Desire To Know Him More Because Of You?

Here is the third question I want you to consider, "How many people have a desire to know Him more because of you?" This question has challenged me to think about the people who I touch on a daily basis. Starting with my wife and kids, my friendships and extended family, with church people, merchants and neighbors, I have had to ask, "How many of them desire to know Him more because of me, my life, and my walk before God?" How many people have I really made homesick for God?" How many people have been inspired to know Him more, to love Him more, to want to draw more closely to His heart because of me?

The answer to this question is not found in seeing how many people you can count. It is a question that is not about numbers, but about your walk with Jesus. It is the fruits of your walk that will impact the lives of others. As they see Jesus in you they will desire to know Him more. This does not mean that unless you are perfect, others will not desire to know Him more. It means that you are walking in sincerity and truth, admitting when you are wrong, asking for forgiveness when necessary, but through it all desiring to be a reflection of the person of Jesus Christ. People are not looking to you for perfection, but they are looking to you for the heart of God to be flowing through your life. It is from that flow that the inspiration will come to others to want to know Him more.

I thank God for every person that He has brought into my life that has planted a desire within me to know Him more. Some of those people I have known for many years, and some I have met for only a few brief moments. Regardless of the length of time that I have known someone, the sweetness of their name and their memory lingers with me because of what was in them. Because of something they spoke to me, I want to know Him more; because of a passion I saw within them, I want to know Him more; because of what they did in a given moment, I want to know Him more. It is from the lives of those who are daily walking as true children of God that the desire to want to know Him more is created in others. Isn't that why we are here? To glorify Him, yes. To enjoy Him forever, yes. But we are also here, as a top priority, to be a reflection of the person of Jesus Christ here on earth.

THE ABBA CRY